D0710254

THE MASS

THE MASS

CARDINAL
JEAN-MARIE LUSTIGER

Translated from the French
by Rebecca Howell Balinski

1817

Harper & Row, Publishers, San Francisco

Cambridge, Hagerstown, New York, Philadelphia, Washington
London, Mexico City, São Paulo, Singapore, Sydney

Acknowledgment is made to the following for permission to reprint copyrighted material: Excerpts from the New American Bible, copyright © 1970 by the Confraternity of Christian Doctrine, Washington, DC, and used with permission. Excerpts from the English translation of *The Roman Missal* © 1973, International Committee on English in the Liturgy, Inc. All rights reserved.

This work was originally published in the French language under the title *La Messe*.

Library of Congress Cataloging-in-Publication Data

Lustiger, Jean-Marie, 1926–
    The Mass.

    1. Mass – Meditations.   2. Lord's Supper (Liturgy) –
Meditations.   3. Catholic Church – Liturgy – Meditations.
I. Title.
BX2169.L87   1987   264'.02036   87-45188
ISBN 0-06-254831-X (pbk.)

87 88 89 90 91 MOY 10 9 8 7 6 5 4 3 2 1

CONTENTS

TRANSLATOR'S NOTE

In the spring and summer of 1985, Cardinal Jean-Marie Lustiger, archbishop of Paris, devoted thirteen of his weekly talks on Radio Notre-Dame to the purpose of "helping Christians to enter more profoundly into the holy feast of the Mass." The following texts were translated from excerpts of these talks, which were printed in *Paris Notre-Dame,* the weekly bulletin of the archdiocese of Paris.

Rebecca Howell Balinski

From age to age you gather a people to yourself
so that from east to west
a perfect offering may be made
to the glory of your name.

CONVOCATION OF THE BAPTIZED

From time to time, perhaps, Christians need to be reminded that it is not just once a year on Easter Sunday but on *every* Sunday that, through the Eucharist, we celebrate the Resurrection of Christ. The Eucharist is a memorial of humanity's redemption, and the essential point to remember about it is this: it is the *resurrected* Christ who convokes and unites us for this sacrifice of thanksgiving. "Come, eat of my bread and drink of the wine I have mixed," Wisdom proclaims in the Old Testament (Prov. 9:5). Wisdom personified is the Word of God.

Participation in the weekly celebration of the Eucharist is an act of faith that draws each of us out of isolation and joins us with a people united in Christ. Therefore, we must beware of treating churches as we would cafeterias or supermarkets that present a variety of foods and merchandise to suit the individual tastes and convenience of their "customers."

As Christians, we go to Mass not because we simply "feel like going"; nor do we go to satisfy our personal sensibilities. We go because Christ calls us, the Holy Spirit gathers us, and God commands it. We go to receive there our dignity as children of God, and to receive as well the strength to live in Christ.

To be a part of the congregation at the Sunday Mass is a grace from God, who brings together his children from all sides and shapes them into the body of Christ.

Each parish community reveals its particular character at the Sunday Mass because those who are gathered there have not chosen each other, but *all have been chosen by God*. In contrast to a monastic community, which celebrates the Mass with its members only, the parish church keeps all doors open. In so doing, it proclaims that the Mass is an act of the church to which all the faithful are called. All of the faithful have the right to participate, and all have the *same* rights, regardless of their differences from society's point of view. At the celebration of the Eucharist, all of us find ourselves before our Lord and Master, who made himself servant of all. Remember the parable of the guests at the marriage feast that the king gave for his son (cf. Matt. 22:1–14)! The only requisite for taking part in the Eucharist is the "wedding garment" that each Christian puts on at the time of Baptism. The Mass is the gathering of the baptized.

The announcement of the gospel to those who are ignorant of it is not the primary purpose of the eucharistic celebration. The Eucharist is, first and foremost, the sacrament of the baptized and confirmed, who have already entered into the mystery of the Church through the sacraments of Christian initiation, of those who have been "born again." In times past, catechumens, although already inscribed on the list of Baptism, attended only the beginning of the Mass; at the Offertory, like great penitents, they humbly left the congregation.

The Eucharist is intended for those who, having been baptized, are identified with Christ crucified and resurrected. From the moment of Baptism we enter fully into communion with Christ, that profound mystery of mercy and grace, who gives himself to his brothers and sisters in order to unite them by his sacrifice.

The Church cannot ask a person, "Are you rich or poor? What language do you speak? What

are your tastes? Who are your friends?" There is
only one valid question: "Do you belong to
Christ?" If so, then you have the right to receive
the Body of Christ, and you also have the right—
and the responsibility—to "receive" your neighbor.
You may have previously ignored your neighbor;
but that person is a gift from God, a brother or a
sister whom you did not expect to find. The joy
of Christian brotherhood is an integral part of the
eucharistic celebration, and it illustrates what the
Church is: the body of Christ.

Finally, the Mass can take place only if there is
present someone who participates in the apostolic succession. The necessary presence of an
ordained minister, a bishop, or a priest permits
God's people to recognize that Christ himself is
active in the sacrament.

Through the ministry and faithfulness of our
ordained brothers, the Church never ceases to
recognize itself and to receive itself as the body of
Christ in each celebration of the Eucharist.

Look with favor on these offerings
and accept them as once you accepted
the gifts of your servant Abel,
the sacrifice of Abraham, our father in faith,
and the bread and wine offered by your priest
  Melchisedech.

WHAT JESUS DOES

Whereas various forms of entertainment, public meetings, and even family celebrations must be forever seeking novelty to arouse interest, we know when we enter a church for a Mass that, in spite of transformations that have occurred across the centuries, we shall find a liturgy whose form has been fixed.

The eucharistic celebration is, in effect, a "codified act" in its reference to Jesus. It makes present that which Jesus himself accomplished once and for all time and that which he does not cease to accomplish for men and women in every age. Today, at the end of the twentieth century, we are neither more nor less distant from Jesus than were the early churches of Rome and Corinth. It is not the time that has passed since his resurrection that measures the distance of Christians from Christ!

Through the Church, Jesus gives to each succeeding generation what he gave to the twelve disciples: "I received from the Lord what I handed on to you, namely, that the Lord Jesus on the night in which he was betrayed took bread . . ." (1 Cor. 11:23). The gestures and words of the celebration signify this fact.

It is important to remember that the gestures and words of Jesus at the Last Supper can be understood only in relation to Mary, his mother, who was steeped in the Jewish religious tradition. It was she who taught Jesus to pray and she who instructed him in the "paths of the Lord" and the "treasures of Heaven" of which Jesus, Son of God and Son of Mary, is the "fullness" (Col. 1:19; Eph. 1:23), the "heir" (Matt. 21:38; Heb. 1:2; Gal. 4:1–7), and the "witness" (Rev. 1:5).

We celebrate the Mass by doing, in our turn, what Jesus did at the Last Supper when he followed the ritual for the Jewish Sabbath and Passover meals. Jesus prayed in the way that the people of Israel prayed, a way that through him became the Christian way of praying. The Lord's Prayer, for example, is based on the ritual prayer of the seventeen benedictions that Jesus learned in childhood and later recast in a unique and personal style.

The Eucharist combines in a single and com-

pletely original celebration two distinct forms of
Jewish rituals in which Jesus took part throughout his lifetime. One form, the liturgy of the synagogue, brings together each Jewish community
on the Sabbath in particular and on special holidays. It includes readings from the Word of God,
chosen according to a predetermined cycle, the
singing of psalms, and the chanting of prayers of
supplication and benediction.

The Jewish model for the Christian liturgy of
the Word is presented to us by the evangelist
Luke (Luke 4:16–22) who recounts that in the
synagogue of Nazareth, the scroll of the prophet
Isaiah was given to Jesus to read: "The spirit of
the Lord is upon me; therefore he has anointed
me. He has sent me to bring glad tidings to the
poor" (Luke 4:18). Then Jesus said, "Today this
Scripture passage is fulfilled in your hearing"
(Luke 4:21). He pronounced the Word, and
then announced its accomplishment.

The rituals for the Sabbath meal and the more
solemn Passover feast represent another form of
Jewish celebration on which the Eucharist is
based. "Where will you have us prepare for you to
eat the Passover?" the Apostles asked Jesus, who
observed the venerable and unchanging ritual of

the deliverance of the people of Israel from Egypt (Exod. 12). The memorial of the Passover was at that time already more than a thousand years old, and was highly charged with emotion and history. For this reason, the innovations that Jesus brought to the ritual are all the more significant and, indeed, surprising.

The Passover feast was a family meal at which the Passover lamb, sacrificed at the Temple, was eaten. It began with the Jewish father's blessing of the unleavened bread in the form of wafers (hosts), which have become a part of the Church's special celebrations. After breaking the bread into small pieces and distributing it to his family, he spoke these words: "This is the bread of misery that our fathers ate in Egypt." Jesus, taking on the role of the father, will say to his new family: "This is my body, which will be given up for you." Acclamations, prayers, and thanksgiving followed. Then, at the end of the meal, there was the blessing of the last glass of wine, which recalled the sacrifice of the lamb in the Temple. The head of the family said: "Blessed art thou, O Lord our God, king of the universe, who createst the fruit of the vine." Jesus will say: "For this is my blood, the blood of the Covenant, to be poured out

in behalf of many for the forgiveness of sins"
(Matt. 26:28).

The distinctive feature of the Christian liturgy—
that is to say, the changes that Christ brought to
it—is that parts of the liturgy of the synagogue—
the act of thanksgiving and the hearing of the
Word—have been combined with the ritual for
the feast of the Passover, and all point to Christ:
it is he who gives us the Word of God, and he is
himself the Word made flesh. It is Jesus who,
speaking to us from the gospel, says through the
mouth of the celebrant, "This is my body; this is
my blood." There is a marvelous spiritual and
sacramental unity in the Mass: the liturgy of the
Word is a eucharistic liturgy, and the eucharistic
liturgy is a liturgy of the Word.

Priest: *In the name of the Father, and of the Son, and of the Holy Spirit.*

People: *Amen.*

THE PEOPLE BECOME THE
TEMPLE OF GOD

If the liturgy of the Word were to be disassociated from the liturgy of the Eucharist, the original character of the Mass would be destroyed. Moreover, a single ecclesiastical "site" is used for the performance of two different rites: the liturgy of the Word, which has its roots in the synagogical ritual (a community celebration), and the eucharistic liturgy, which is based on the rituals for the Sabbath and Passover meals (family celebrations).

The essential and specific unity of the Christian ceremony—Christ speaks through the Word *and* offers himself in the eucharistic feast—is made clear by the role of the celebrant, an ordained minister (a bishop, who is a successor to the Apostles, or a priest who shares his sacramental mission). The minister is the sign of the presence of Christ in his Church.

Although the celebrant of the Eucharist is always a priest, all priests who are present at the

Mass are not celebrants. Because there is only one Christ, Lord of the Church, a group of priests cannot preside as a collective. All priests concelebrate the Mass inasmuch as they are priests; however, only one among them, from the beginning to the end, officiates. He is the "principal" celebrant in the etymological sense. He represents the "Principle" who is Christ, "head of the body," which is his Church (Col. 1:18). He speaks for Christ, who summons the baptized in order to give them his Word and his Body.

In order for a Christian congregation to become what it ought to be (i.e., the body of Christ), a minister of the Church must carry out the "capital" mission for which he has been designated by God (cf. Heb. 5:10): the priestly act of celebrating the Eucharist.

The Entrance Song

It is the Entrance Song that allows a gathering of individual Christians to take form. People sing with fellow worshipers words of praise, penitence, or supplication addressed to God. By this common spiritual activity, the men and women assembled in the church, and up until that moment lacking cohesion, become a community of adoration and prayer.

In the tradition of the Western church, the Entrance Song is usually one of 150 psalms, which give us "the words to express God." The Psalms, when learned by heart, become our own words – a mother tongue with which we can speak to God. Unless we learn the language of God, we risk remaining completely inarticulate.

The celebrant, therefore, enters into the midst of people already united by song. His entry is much more than a ceremonial or solemn act; it is a reminder of the entrance of Jesus, the Messiah, into the Temple (Luke 2:22–50; 19:47; 21:37; 22:53; Zech. 6:12). Thus, the faithful are made aware that *they* have become the holy temple, inhabited by the Spirit. They become a true temple made of living stones, where Christ will manifest his presence while associating their praise with his Word and his sacrifice.

Peter writes: "Come to him, a living stone, rejected by men but approved, nonetheless, and precious in God's eyes. You too are like living stones, built as an edifice of spirit, into a holy priesthood, offering spiritual sacrifices acceptable to God through Jesus Christ" (1 Pet. 2:4–5).

Having entered the congregation, the celebrant, before speaking a word, steps up to the altar and kisses it. The kissing of the altar, which in the first Christian communities was the tomb of the martyrs, signifies that everything is submitted to Christ: the altar, the priest, and the victim (Heb. 9:14) who is present at the gathering.

After this expression of veneration, sometimes accompanied by incense, the presiding priest turns to the people and says: "In the name of the Father, and of the Son, and of the Holy Spirit." The Sign of the Cross, which each worshiper makes along with the priest, is the community's initial profession of faith in the mystery of God. It proclaims the identity of the "convened," who are united in their response to the priest: "Amen."

Priest: *The Lord be with you.*

People: *And also with you.*

4

THE FIRST BENEDICTION

When he greets the faithful, the celebrant, a brother surrounded by brothers and sisters, speaks in the name of Christ. His greeting is far from a banal "Good morning." It is a benediction that sums up the entire history of salvation. In the assembled church, the priest and the congregation recognize each other by these words of benediction. Among the expressions proposed by the liturgy, I give precedence to two: "The Lord be with you" and "Peace be with you."

"The Lord be with you" is most likely one of the oldest of benedictions. It can be found on almost every page of the Bible. The liturgical language uses "Lord" (the Latin, *Dominus;* the Greek, *Kyrie;* and the Hebrew, *Adonai*) in order to respect the name of God revealed to Moses: "I am who I am" (Exod. 3:14). "The Lord be with you" is not a wish. It is a benediction that recognizes that God himself is present in the midst of his people. God, in revealing his "name" to us and in giving us the secret of his intimacy, makes his dwelling place among us.

Jesus, at the end of his earthly life, says to the Apostles, "And know that I am with you always, until the end of the world" (Matt. 28:20). The eternal Son of God made man, the Word made flesh, announces that henceforth he will dwell in the holy temple that is the Church, a new people brought together by the Spirit.

"Peace be with you" is a customary salutation among the people of Israel: "I will hear what God proclaims; / the Lord—for he proclaims peace. / To his people, and to his faithful ones, / and to those who put in him their hope" (Ps. 85:9).

God's peace implies the fullness of life with him and the joy of living among brothers and sisters. God, present among his people, transfigures all human life.

The Messiah, "Prince of Peace" (Isa. 9:5), who came to "guide our feet into the way of peace" (Luke 1:79), confides to his Apostles at the Last Supper, "'Peace' is my farewell to you, my peace is my gift to you; I do not give it to you as the world gives peace" (John 14:27; cf. 16:33). The resurrected Christ appears with these words: "Peace be with you. . . . As the Father has sent

me, so I send you. . . . Receive the Holy Spirit"
(John 20:21–22).

Thus, it is in the name of Christ that the celebrant greets the people. Notice that he says,
"Peace be with *you*," or, "The Lord be with *you*,"
and not "with *us*," as every priest would be
tempted to say and every one of the faithful to
think. The celebrant is not, however, the spokes-
man for the people, not that he excludes himself
from them or stands aloof. His duty, which he
performs with the courage that comes from his
"mission," is to let Christ speak through his lips
to the Church.

At the moment when the priest pronounces
the greeting that is destined for himself as well as
for the congregation, he receives it in the same act
of faith required of each Christian assembled for
the Eucharist: we believe that Christ is present
and that he has brought us together by his Spirit
so that we can give thanks to the Father.

The liturgy suggests several expressions of
salutation, many of which are taken from the
beginnings or endings of Paul's letters. They are
all beautiful and express the mystery of the
Trinity and the gift of peace.

After the benediction, it is up to the priest to introduce the people to the eucharistic sacrifice by words that often refer to the theme of the day's celebration (feast days, mysteries of the life of Christ or the Virgin, remembrance of certain saints, etc.). However, the introduction to the day's Mass *always* gives emphasis to the Word of God, especially to the Gospel reading for the day.

Supported by the faith of the Church and nourished by the Scriptures, the celebrant then invites the congregation to enter into the heart of the revealed mystery. He has the charge of expressing in his introductory remarks, on a specific day and at a specific Mass, the focus for the prayer of the assembled congregation.

I confess to almighty God,
and to you, my brothers and sisters,
that I have sinned through my own fault
in my thoughts and in my words,
in what I have done,
and in what I have failed to do;
and I ask blessed Mary, ever virgin,
all the angels and saints,
and you, my brothers and sisters,
to pray for me to the Lord our God.

$$\overline{5}$$

THE CONFESSION OF OUR SINS

The people enter into the eucharistic celebration by asking for the grace of a "contrite heart." At the moment when the Lord of Holiness brings us together in order to share the fullness of his life, we are invited to recognize that we have sinned and that, hence, we belong to a people of sinners whom Christ has sanctified. This confession does not replace the sacrament of Penance. However, the grace of the Eucharist purifies us from our turning away from God, so long as our sins have not produced a mortal rupture.

The Penitential Rite

The priest invites the faithful to the penitential act, a returning of our hearts to God by saying, for example: "My brothers and sisters, to prepare ourselves to celebrate the sacred mysteries, let us call to mind our sins." Each person then, under the eyes of God, asks this grace:

"Lord, I offer you my life. Give me the sensitivity to feel distressed that I love you so little, to suffer because I so often fail to follow your example. Help me to discover my sin. Give me a contrite heart."

A period of silence at this time allows the secret prayers of individuals to become the unique prayer of the assembled.

The celebrant then asks the people to recall their sins in a public prayer. One of the oldest forms of the prayer used in the Penitential Rite begins: "I confess to almighty God. . . ."

To confess our sins is both to acknowledge and to recognize them, to face the truth about our lives. Each of us is responsible for his or her acts, and we acknowledge that responsibility before others. First of all, we confess to God. "Against thee, thee only, have I sinned" is repeated in Ps. 51:4 as an echo of the confession of David. It is the love of God that judges us because sin is the refusal of God's love and, thus, the rejection of God, who is the source of our love for our brothers and sisters.

"I confess . . . and to you, my brothers and sisters," who are the Church, "that I have sinned through my own fault" (at this point we strike our breasts) "in my thoughts and in my words, in what I have done, and in what I have failed to do." Every area of human freedom and activity is covered in this public admission.

There follows a supplication that is addressed to "blessed Mary, ever virgin," the first person from the Church to be saved, and to "all the angels and saints," who are the invisible splendor of God, and, finally, to the totality of our brothers and sisters, known and unknown: "Pray for me to the Lord our God."

The priest concludes, "May almighty God have mercy on us, forgive us our sins, and brings us to everlasting life." Notice that the priest says *us* because he is among the sinners and this act of contrition is common to all. On the other hand, in the expression of pardon after the sacrament of Confession, the priest prays, "May almighty God have mercy on *you*." He absolves the penitent and says, "*Your* sins are forgiven."

The Kyrie

After the Penitential Rite comes a brief litany: "Lord, have mercy, Christ, have mercy, Lord, have mercy." It is a translation of a Greek prayer, the Kyrie, which has been preserved not only in the Eastern church, but also in the Latin church, where it was a part of the original liturgy. I prefer this litany in Greek because it is a *witness* to the language in which the New Testament was compiled and that communicated the Word of God to pagan nations for the first time. The Kyrie is a part of a liturgical tradition transmitted from century to century and from nation to nation. It attests to the fact that in spite of their diverse cultures and languages, Christians throughout the world are united in prayer and communion with Christ.

A number of words used in the Mass come from an even older liturgical tradition; they are Hebrew words that have survived intact the various translations of the Old and New Testaments: *Amen* (Yes, it's true!), *Alleluia* (Praise God!), and *Hosannah* (God saves!). These ancient expressions, inserted into our modern liturgies like precious stones, demonstrate the continuity and the catholicity of the Church down through the ages, even though many different people have introduced their own customs, sensibilities, and languages into their manner of praying.

"Lord, have mercy." This prayer, whether turned toward Christ or toward the three divine Persons, is always a supplication *and* an admission of sin.

Glory to God in the highest,
  and peace to his people on earth.
Lord God, heavenly King,
almighty God and Father,
  we worship you, we give you thanks,
  we praise you for your glory.
Lord Jesus Christ, only Son of the Father,
Lord God, Lamb of God,
you take away the sin of the world:
  have mercy on us;
you are seated at the right hand of the Father:
  receive our prayer.
For you alone are the Holy One,
you alone are the Lord,
you alone are the Most High,
  Jesus Christ,
  with the Holy Spirit,
  in the glory of God the Father. Amen.

THE GLORIA AND THE
OPENING PRAYER

Following the admission of sin, the community of faithful unites first to sing a hymn of praise to God and then to listen in silence to the opening prayer, which is spoken by the priest in the name of all those gathered.

The Gloria

On special holidays and Sundays, except during the periods of Advent and Lent, the celebrant begins the hymn "Glory to God," or the Gloria, after the Rite of Penitence. This very old hymn was originally a morning prayer preserved in the *Apostolic Constitutions* (late fourth century). Little by little it was introduced into the eucharistic liturgy. At first, because of its opening words, "Gloria in excelsis Deo," the acclamation of the angels who appeared to the shepherds at Bethlehem after the birth of the Messiah (Luke 2:14), it was reserved for Christmas Masses celebrated by a bishop. Gradually, however, its usage spread to other Masses. Finally, in the eleventh century, the Gloria was incorporated into the eucharistic liturgy, and was sung by everyone as it is today.

This splendid hymn of praise should be sung through without being interrupted by refrains that do not respect its style. It is a poem, not a song to be broken up into "verses" and a "chorus."

The Gloria is a veritable treasure for nourishing personal and communal prayer. It is a prayer of thanksgiving, a eucharistic prayer to God, our Creator and Redeemer. It is, in short, a Magnificat of the Church.

"We worship you, we give you thanks, we praise you for your glory. . . ." Exultation and jubilation flow from our hearts to our lips when we contemplate the immense glory of God, the Almighty Father of the only Son, Lord Jesus Christ. In his humanity, Jesus Christ our Savior receives all the titles of divinity: "Lord God, Lamb of God." This completely worshipful confession of faith becomes a confident supplication toward him who "takes away the sins of the world . . . the Most High, Jesus Christ, with the Holy Spirit, in the glory of God the Father."

On the note of "glory" the swelling voices of the people, overflowing with joy and lyricism, reach the climax of the effusion of praise and adoration. The final "Amen" is a ringing affirmation of faith.

The Opening Prayer

In response to the celebrant, who says, "Let us pray," the people become still and silent.

All turn toward the priest, who speaks the words of the prayer in the name of all the faithful. For that reason, the text is written in the first person plural: "*We* pray. . . ."

According to the rigorously Trinitarian framework of Christian prayer, this orison is addressed *in* the name of Christ, with whom we pray, *by* the Spirit, who gives us strength, *to* "[his] Father and [our] Father" (John 20:17).

The first part of the opening prayer conveys in a phrase of thanksgiving an aspect of the mystery of God: "God who has saved us, who has revealed his love to us, who has done such and such. . . ."

The second part of the prayer is a request that Christians "live from the Source to which they give thanks."

The conclusion situates our prayer very precisely in relation to the Trinity: we petition God the Father *through* the mediation of Christ and *in* the Holy Spirit. We acclaim the Trinitarian mystery that we worship, and we conclude the prayer with a Hebrew expression: ". . . now and for ever and ever." The divine sovereignty that we approach by prayer surpasses every human dimension and plunges us into the culmination of history. The people respond with "Amen," thus affirming the truthfulness of God and the authenticity of their reverent love for him. They, along with the mighty chorus of angels and the innumerable host of the elected, glorify his name: "Amen!" "Praise and glory, wisdom and thanksgiving and honor, power and might, to our God forever and ever. Amen!" (Rev. 7:12).

The words of the prayer that concludes the Introductory Rite in no way reflect the originality of the celebrant. Indeed, it is easy to understand why, according to ancient tradition, the priest always sang this prayer. In so doing, he reinforces the role that he fills in serving the people. The priest is dispossessed of himself in order to articulate the common prayer that dwells in the hearts of the people. Each worshiper should be able to acknowledge the priest's words as his or her own, regardless of sensibility or mood at that moment.

In listening to the opening prayer, whether it is sung or spoken, everyone should be able to say: "By these words pronounced by the priest, it is I who am praying in the name of the Church, and it is the Church that is praying in my name."

Priest: *This is the gospel of the Lord.*

People: *Praise to you, Lord Jesus Christ.*

THE SYMPHONY OF THE WORD OF GOD

At the eucharistic celebrations on Sundays and feast days, there are three readings from the Holy Scriptures: a reading from the Old Testament followed by a psalm, a reading from the apostolic writings (Letters from the Apostles or Saint Paul, Revelation, or the Acts of the Apostles), and the proclamation of the Gospel.

The Church responds to these readings in three different ways: by the homily (an actualization of the words of Jesus that, along with the proclamation of the Gospel, is reserved for an ordained minister), by the profession of its baptismal faith, and, finally, by the Prayer of the Faithful for all of the Church.

The relationship of the three readings to each other illustrates the interlocking structure of the divine revelation. The Word of God resounds like a spiritual symphony in which each harmony makes it easier to perceive the beauty and significance of the whole.

The Gospel

In the Gospel, it is Christ himself, Word of God made flesh, who speaks to the Church. The people stand when the Gospel is read, not only out of respect, but, more significantly, in order to announce the coming of the resurrected Jesus into the gathering of his brothers and sisters, whom he will one day resurrect. Standing, we salute the entry of Christ with the Alleluia.

The fact that the Gospel is read by an ordained minister, a priest, or a deacon signifies that in the evangelistic Word, the living Christ speaks to us. Hence, the final acclamation: "Praise to you, Lord Jesus Christ!"

The First and Second Readings

The "melody" of the Gospel is heard best, however, against the background of a symphony composed of melodies from three other parts of the Word of God. In effect, there is a progressive revelation in the liturgy of the Word. As Saint Gregory Nazianzen said, "The Old Testament clearly manifests the Father, but only obscurely the Son. The New Testament reveals the Son and insinuates the divinity of the Spirit. Today the Spirit dwells among us and He makes himself clearly known."

There exists a historic, prophetic, and sacramental connection between the revelation of God given to Moses and to the prophets in the Old Testament, and the Son, Word of God made flesh.

The Church never ceases to give thanks for this revelation. It sings the Magnificat with the Virgin Mary: "He has upheld Israel his servant, ever mindful of his mercy; Even as he promised our fathers, promised Abraham and his descendants forever" (Luke 1:54–55). The voice of the Father is heard at the time of the Transfiguration: "This is my beloved Son on whom my favor rests. Listen to him" (Matt. 17:5). Jesus reveals the Father: "Whoever has seen me has seen the Father" (John 14:9). If we are to hear Jesus speaking in the Gospels, we must have heard and understood *beforehand* the Word of the Father. The readings that precede the Gospel are not intended to clarify it, but rather to lead us into the history of salvation, into the mystery of God, of the Son, and of the Spirit.

The original and specific writings of the Apostles, heard as they are between the Old Testament and the Gospel, present us with the witness to the Holy Spirit at work in the apostolic generation. The spirit speaks through the Apostles, who witness to Christ. Because of their words, we are able to recognize the gift that is made to us by the Father: the Spirit who lives in our hearts.

The Responsorial Psalm

The Psalm provides the connection between the three readings in which we hear respectively words inspired by the Father in the Old Testament, echoes of the Holy Spirit in the apostolic writings, and the voice of Jesus Christ himself in the Gospel. The Psalms are treasures polished over the centuries by the prayers of the people of Israel, the prayers of Jesus and the Apostles, and the prayers of the Church—from its beginning "until the end of time."

The Psalms are "a resumé of all Scripture" and are the best spiritual initiation to both the Old and New Testaments. Whoever learns to pray with them will afterward, when "wandering" through the Bible, be surprised to "understand" God speaking. (It is an experience common to monks who are steeped in the Psalter.)

In short, the Psalms brings our hearts into harmony with the song of God.

Priest: *Blessed are you, Lord, God of all creation. Through your goodness we have this bread to offer, which earth has given and human hands have made. It will become for us the bread of life.*

People: *Blessed be God for ever.*

8

THE CHURCH'S RESPONSE

 The readings for the Sunday Mass are a part of a three-year cycle, just as in the synagogical liturgy that Christ knew. They are chosen solely from Scripture, never from a spiritual author, a Church Father, or even an encyclical, all of which can be read in the celebration of the Liturgy of Hours. The Eucharist is not an ordinary celebration or reunion for prayer in which we can take a free initiative. It is *an act of the church* that has been brought together by the Holy Spirit. It is the celebration in which Christ shares himself with us through the Word of God, his Father, and through his Body and Blood.

The Church responds to the three readings by the homily of the priest, by its Profession of Faith, and by the Prayer of the Faithful.

The Homily

The homily is an integral part of the proclamation of the Gospel. For this reason, it is always given by an ordained minister (a priest or a bishop), and preferably it is given by the same priest who celebrates the Eucharist. The homily is neither a catechistic lesson nor an expression of the minister's personal views about life – nor is it a test of eloquence. It is a strict and unequivocal *mission:* the priest has the task of making meaningful to the particular group of people before him the Word of Christ that he has just proclaimed.

The act of faith required of the people who listen to the homily is just as necessary as that required of the priest who is fulfilling his mission. Remember the admonishment of Jesus after one of his sermons in parable: "Let everyone heed what he hears!" (Matt. 13:9).

The Profession of Faith

The Profession of Faith, or Credo, of the Church is repeated every Sunday because every Sunday we celebrate the Resurrection of the Lord. In its recitation we recall the Resurrection and Christian Baptism. The words of the Profession of Faith have their origin in the triple interrogation that in the early church preceded each of the three immersions of a catechumen in the baptismal water. "Do you believe in God the Father? . . . in Jesus Christ, his son? . . . in the Holy Spirit?" After each question the catechumen responded, "I believe." The recitation of the Credo is, thus, a sign of recognition among Christians, and a reminder of our personal Baptisms. The proclamation of these words, which were made into a fixed creed by an undivided church (that is to say, before the great schisms), unites us, in spite of our "little faith," in the baptismal faith of the Church throughout the world and over the centuries.

The Prayer of the Faithful

The Prayer of the Faithful embraces the entire Church and becomes the supplication of all Christians everywhere. The general intercession of Good Friday with its ten intentions is the model for this prayer, aptly called "universal," which originated in the early church.

The Offertory

After the three responses to God's Word, we enter into the eucharistic sacrifice itself, which begins with the Offertory. At this point in the Mass, take a moment to observe the altar, the sacred table of Christ's sacrifice and a symbol of him. It is not a simple piece of furniture. Its beauty and purity require that nothing be placed there except the necessary and significant objects, such as a candle whose flame symbolizes the resurrected Christ, light of the world. The missal, which is there to aid the memory of the celebrant, should be discreetly placed.

As the celebrant prepares the bread and wine that have been brought to the altar by members of the congregation, the people offer their gifts. It is entirely appropriate that this offering should be made at this point in the Mass: the gift that each Christian makes, far from being the price of a seat or a kind of tax, is a concrete sign of fraternal love. It allows the faithful to participate in the material life of the Church and to share with those in need.

Our gifts are also an expression of the fact that we are united with Christ at the moment of the presentation of the bread and the wine, which will become his Body and his Blood. Even so, money is not an element of the sacrament, as are the bread and wine.

Through him,
with him,
in him,
in the unity of the Holy Spirit,
all glory and honor is yours,
almighty Father,
for ever and ever.

9

THE EUCHARISTIC PRAYER

The part of the eucharistic celebration in which the bread and the wine, elements of the sacrifice of Christ, are presented by the celebrant is called the Offertory. Pay close attention to what the priest says and what he does.

The Preparation of the Gifts

You will note that a drop of water is mixed with the wine. This practice goes back to a Jewish ritual that Jesus followed. The prayers recited by the priest when presenting the bread and the wine are Jewish benedictions that were pronounced daily before the family meal: "Blessed are you, Lord, God of all creation. Through your goodness we have this bread to offer. . . ."

After the preparation of the gifts (oblats), the priest purifies his hands, not as a practical gesture of cleanliness, but rather as an observance of a penitential rite also retained from the Jewish liturgy (Matt. 15:2; 20; Mark 7:2; Luke 11:38). As the Psalmist recalls, "I wash my hands in innocence, / and I go around your altar, O Lord" (Ps. 26:6).

All the prayers of the Offertory can be said in a low voice by the celebrant while each member of the congregation prays silently. Why, you may ask, are certain prayers repeated in a low voice while others are said aloud? The answer is that the importance of certain parts of the liturgical action requires that prayers be pronounced in such a way that everyone can hear and understand the words.

Hence, the prayer over the bread and the wine at the conclusion of the Offertory is spoken aloud. Notice that this is true for the completion of each "part" of the Mass, from the Introductory Rite to the prayer that comes at the end of the Communion Rite and in which the priest sums up what the people have just experienced and, in their name, gives thanks and implores that "we may live the life of faith since we have been strengthened by Christ himself."*

---

* *Celebrating the Eucharist* (Collegeville, Minn.: Liturgical Press, 1986), 21.

The Eucharistic Prayer

The Eucharistic Prayer begins with a three-part dialogue, which introduces its "preface," between the celebrant and the people.

Priest: *The Lord be with you.*
People: *And also with you.*

Priest: *Lift up your hearts.*
People: *We lift them up to the Lord.*

Priest: *Let us give thanks to the Lord our God.*
People: *It is right to give him thanks and praise.*

It ends with the people's "Amen" after the concluding doxology, which renders glory and honor to the almighty Father *through* Christ, *with* Christ, *in* Christ, "in the unity of the Holy Spirit."

Whereas in the liturgy of the Word, the participation of the congregation is varied in form, during the Eucharistic Prayer, there is an almost face-to-face relationship between the celebrant, who acts "in persona Christi-Capitis" (in the person of Christ, head of the Church), and the people brought together by the Holy Spirit to be the body of Christ.

At four separate times during the Eucharistic Prayer, the faithful express verbally their union with the sacrifice of Christ. After the opening dialogue mentioned above comes the Sanctus ("Holy, Holy, Holy Lord"), which is chanted or sung with the celebrant, who alone proclaims the preface preceding it. (The words of the preface vary according to the liturgical calendar.) The third "intervention" occurs after the consecration of the bread and the wine when the people join the celebrant in proclaiming "the mystery of the faith," or reminiscence, with a burst of adoration in memory of Christ: "Christ has died, Christ has risen, Christ will come again." Finally, the congregation responds with "Amen" at the end of the doxology ("Through him, with him, in him . . . for ever and ever"), which is repeated in its entirety by the priest alone.

The priest, who becomes a minister of Christ through his ordination, bears witness to and renders Christ present in his Church. Indeed, the tenor of the Eucharistic Prayer leads us to understand this. Note that, with the exception of the reminiscence, the prayer is always addressed to the Father, and that it ends in the name of Christ: "Through him, with him, in him. . . ." By these words Christ unites his Church to his sacrifice. It is the priest who, in celebrating the Eucharist, the sacerdotal mission for which he was ordained, makes it possible for the Church to enter into this unique relationship with Christ, its Lord.

Three prayers, all of them said *after* the consecration of the bread and the wine and with Communion in mind, are addressed directly to Christ, who sacrifices himself for his Church.

The first of these prayers, the acclamation of the people recalling their salvation – the reminiscence – is, as just pointed out, a part of the Eucharistic Prayer. The second is a prayer for peace, which immediately precedes the Sign of Peace. It is the first of three prayers that used to be said privately by the priest in the humble attitude of a faithful servant who is about to receive the Body of Christ. Today, the celebrant prays aloud in the name of all the people: "Lord Jesus Christ . . . Look not on *our* sins, but on the faith of your Church." Finally, the litany of the Agnus Dei is chanted by the people just before Communion: "Lamb of God, you take away the sins of the world: have mercy on us. Lamb of God, you take away the sins of the world: have mercy on us. Lamb of God, you take away the sins of the world: grant us peace."

On the night he was betrayed,
he took bread and gave you thanks and praise.
He broke the bread, gave it to his disciples, and said:
Take this, all of you, and eat it:
this is my body which will be given up for you.
When supper was ended, he took the cup.
Again he gave you thanks and praise,
gave the cup to his disciples, and said:
Take this, all of you, and drink from it:
this is the cup of my blood,
the blood of the new and everlasting covenant.
It will be shed for you and for all
so that sins may be forgiven.

10

A SACRIFICE OF THANKSGIVING

Who actually speaks during the Eucharistic Prayer?

The *priest* speaks. Note that with one exception, he always uses the first person plural, "we," because he speaks for all of the Church, the totality of the body of Christ. He addresses himself to our Heavenly Father using the second person familiar, "Thee . . . thou," and he refers to Christ in the third person: "On the night *He* was betrayed, *He* took bread. . . ."

There is one part of the prayer, however, where the priest speaks in the first person singular. He does this to allow Christ himself to pronounce the same words that he used at the institution of the Eucharist: "This is *my* body. . . . Do this in memory of *me*."

Through the ministry of the priest, the unique sacrifice of Christ is made sacramentally present to the Church at every Mass. Although the Mass is a true sacrifice, it can never be the equivalent of Christ's sacrifice made on the cross.

Throughout the Eucharistic Prayer, Christ, the Church, and the priest speak and act together with an indissoluble bond. How deep is the mystery we enter!

The Eucharist is a prayer of thanksgiving for our salvation. Hence, it requires a total offering of ourselves: our freedom, our intelligence, and our hearts. In short, we are to offer all of those qualities that make us creatures of God, capable of receiving and reciprocating love.

The Eucharist is a sacrifice made holy by God. It is a "making sacred," as Saint Augustine said. Above all, it is a gesture of love. It reverses the inroads of sin, which is a refusal to give thanks, and, thus, it reconciles us with God. The prophets of the Old Testament stressed over and over again the meaning of sacrificial worship: "For it is love that I desire, not sacrifice, and knowledge of God rather than holocausts" (Hos. 6:6). The true sacrifice desired by God is "a contrite spirit; a heart contrite and humbled" (Ps. 51:19), which reconstructs what sin has destroyed.

"Sacrifice or oblation you wished not, / but ears open to obedience you gave me. / Holocausts or sin-offerings you sought not; / then said I,

'Behold I come; / in the written scroll it is prescribed for me, / To do your will, O my God, is my delight, / and your law is within my heart.'" These words of the Psalmist (Ps. 40:7–9) are precisely those used by Christ when he came into the world (Heb. 10:5–7).

In offering himself as a sacrifice in the act of thanksgiving, Jesus fulfills the supreme act of the only Son of God, of the Word made flesh. He is Savior and Redeemer who delivers man from his sin and brings him into full communion with God. Thus, another of Saint Augustine's definitions of sacrifice is verified: The sacrifice of Jesus "contributes toward the great blessing of uniting us with God in a holy society."

Who makes the offering at the Eucharist?

First of all, it is *Christ* who, in his Church, offers himself to the Father for the salvation of mankind. He offers himself as nourishment for his brothers and sisters: "Take this . . . and eat it." The new and eternal covenant has been sealed by his blood.

Second, it is the *priest* who, as a minister both of Christ and of the Church, offers sacramentally. That is the significance of his raising up at the same time the bread, Body of Christ, and the wine, shed Blood of Christ, at the end of the Eucharistic Prayer. This sacrifice of Christ to the glory of his Father is offered by the priest in the name of the assembled congregation, which unites itself with the sacrifice by its acclamation of "Amen!"

Who is offered?

It is *Christ* who is offered. Although he has made the unique offering once and for all time (Heb. 9:26–28), he is present at the Mass in his Body and in his Blood.

The *Church,* the body of Christ, is also offered along with Christ as head, through him, with him, and in him: "Look with favor on your Church's offering, and see the Victim whose death has reconciled us to yourself."

Finally, it is *all of us,* individual members of the body of Christ, who are offered and who offer ourselves "as a living sacrifice, holy and acceptable to God" according to the words used by Saint Paul to exhort the Christians of Rome to live a "spiritual worship" (Rom. 12:1).

In the act of Christ at the Mass, thanksgiving *and* sacrifice are united and fulfilled. "By one offering he has forever perfected those who are being sanctified. The Holy Spirit attests this to us, for after saying, 'This is the covenant that I will make with them after those days, says the Lord: I will put my laws in their hearts and I will write them on their minds,' he also says, 'Their sins and their transgressions I will remember no more.' Once these have been forgiven, there is no further offering for sin" (Heb. 10:14–18).

Father, calling to mind the death your Son endured
  for our salvation,
his glorious resurrection and ascension into heaven,
and ready to greet him when he comes again,
we offer you in thanksgiving this holy and living
  sacrifice.
Look with favor on your Church's offering,
and see the Victim whose death has reconciled us to
  yourself.

"DO THIS IN MEMORY OF ME"

In celebrating the Mass, we repeat the gestures and words used by Jesus on the evening of his last Passover observed with the twelve Apostles according to the Jewish liturgical tradition. All of Christian liturgical tradition follows the model of Jesus' prayer on that evening. He first gave thanks to the Father Creator, then recalled the wonders of Israel's salvation, and, finally, he climaxed the ritual by the offering of his body, "given up for you," and of his "blood of the Covenant" shed "for you and for all men so that sins may be forgiven."

Therefore, the Mass is, in effect, *two* "memorials" of mankind's redemption: it is the memorial of the Passover of Israel, celebrated by Jesus, joined with the memorial of the Passover of Jesus, which we celebrate "in memory of him" as he asked his Apostles to do. Through this memorial we receive today the salvation that was given to us "once for all" (Heb. 9:27) by Christ through his sacrifice, and we also receive the hope that this salvation will be completed at the end of time.

The dialogue before the preface of the Eucharistic Prayer and the Sanctus, which is afterward sung in unison by the congregation, are both parts of the Passover ritual.

"Holy, holy, holy Lord, God of power and might."

These words rang out in the ears of Isaiah when in the Temple the glory of God and his own vocation as prophet were revealed to him (Is. 6:3). The invisible creatures of God sang his praises with a mighty chorus of overwhelming joy; their words acclaimed the holiness of God, Lord of the universe, the holiness of the Creator, who holds all things in his powerful hand; and they extolled his merciful love.

"Blessed is he who comes in the name of the Lord."

This messianic acclamation taken from Ps. 118 (v. 26) set the tempo for the entrance procession at the feast of Tabernacles. It was jubilantly repeated by the crowds of people waving palm branches when Jesus entered Jerusalem: "Hosanna to the

Son of David! Blessed is he who comes in the name of the Lord! Hosanna in the highest!" (Matt. 21:9).

In the Christian liturgy, these two passages of Scripture from Isaiah and the Psalms have been combined with striking force and coherence to become an irreplaceable element of the Eucharistic Prayer. When the congregation, made up of sinful and mortal people, uses these words in glorifying Jesus, Son and Messiah, it praises God with a stirring hymn that, even when sung by only a handful of the faithful, resounds throughout creation and in the ears of a redeemed humanity united in its adoration of the "church of the heavens."

On the evening of the Last Supper, Jesus gave thanks and praise to God, his Father and our Father. In following the Passover ritual he recalled the entire history of salvation: the Creation, God's promise to Abraham, the deliverance of Israel from Egypt, the gift of the Covenant with its call to God's holiness, the presence of God in his Temple, and the promise of the Messiah, savior of all people who would be called to become the children of the Son. Furthermore, it was in following the ritual, which would thereafter become sacramental for Christians, that Jesus through love offered up himself "in this bread," sacrament of his body given up for us, and "in this wine," sacrament of his blood shed for the multitude.

Thus, Jesus gave to his Apostles *beforehand* the sacrament of the sacrifice that he would make by his death on the cross on Friday, of his Resurrection on the third day, and of the gift of the Spirit at Pentecost on the fiftieth day.

Through the Passion of Jesus, who died for our sins and was resurrected for our life, we become from the time of our Baptism new beings belonging to a new people brought together by the Holy Spirit who lives in our hearts. For this reason, we can today and every day repeat the thanksgiving ritual of Jesus and celebrate the sacrifice that he presented to his Father before his Passion.

"Do this in memory of me."

The sacrifice of the Mass includes us in the thanksgiving, the Eucharist, of Jesus. This "memorial" is not a "remembering." By the faith of the Church it becomes an act by which something that happened in the past is given to us in the present. It orients us toward the future of humanity that will "one day" receive Christ in his glory.

Yes, the words and even the gestures used by Jesus almost two thousand years ago are the points to which the Church's fidelity to all that Jesus accomplished in the ensuing three days is anchored. It is just as the apostle Paul wrote to the Christians in Corinth: "I received from the Lord what I handed on to you, namely, that the Lord Jesus on the night in which he was betrayed took bread and after he had given thanks, broke it and said. . ." (1 Cor. 11:23–24).

Grant that we, who are nourished by his body and
    blood,
may be filled with his Holy Spirit,
and become one body, one spirit in Christ.

12

THE HOLY SPIRIT AND
THE BODY OF CHRIST

The Eucharistic Prayer is still called "canon," which means "rule" in Greek, because it conforms to the rule or code of laws of the Church. Therefore, it cannot be altered by subjective fantasy or improvisation. It is a prayer with fixed words and gestures, "ritualized" since the time of Jesus. However, "fixed" does not mean uniform.

From the earliest days of Christianity, the liturgical tradition began to reflect a variety of cultures and languages. That variety was not suppressed by the predominance of the Greek-Byzantine and Latin rites of the churches of the East and the West, respectively, which are, as we were recently reminded by Pope John Paul II, the "lungs" of the Church.

Even within the Latin church, there exist several different rites. The Ambrosian rite is used in Milan; in France, there is the rite of Lyon as well as the rites of the Dominicans and the Chartreux. It was only in the nineteenth century that certain rites particular to specific dioceses were abolished.

There is a lesson to be learned from Saint Methodius, who died just over a thousand years ago, and his brother Cyril. Brought up in the Byzantine culture, they invented an alphabet in order to translate the liturgy of the Church into Slavic languages. They did this with the encouragement of the pope, but in spite of the opposition of the bishops of Germany, who insisted that there were only three languages—Hebrew, Greek, and Latin—acceptable for liturgical use.

Making it possible for a people to pray and understand the marvels of God in its own language is in fact following the Church's long tradition that began at Pentecost. To be shocked by hearing the Mass in one's mother tongue is to ignore Christian history and the manner in which God, by the Holy Spirit, gathers his people from diverse cultures and languages into a single body. The originality of each people enriches the common treasure of the entire Church.

Just as languages vary, so do the forms of the Eucharistic Prayer. In our Latin liturgy there are two major types.

On the one hand, there is Eucharistic Prayer I, a result of the linking of the Roman canon to the Syrian tradition, which developed from the early church at Jerusalem.

On the other, there is Prayer II, taken from Hippolytus of Rome (second and third centuries), and there are Prayers III and IV, taken from the *Apostolic Constitution* (late fourth century) and recomposed after Vatican II.

I suggest that you take the time to reflect on the words of these prayers. Take Eucharistic Prayer IV, for example. It recounts in a linear way the entire history of salvation, which climaxes with God's gift of his Son, who shed his blood for us. You will note that just before the institution of the Eucharist, the Holy Spirit is invoked for the first time. While spreading his hands over the bread and the wine the priest prays: "Father, may this Holy Spirit sanctify these offerings. Let them become the body and blood of Jesus Christ our Lord as we celebrate the great mystery which He left us as an everlasting covenant." The covenant to which he refers was initiated by God in the Sinai and fulfilled by the Spirit just as Ezekiel and Jeremiah prophesied:

"And I will put my spirit within you and make

you live by my statutes, careful to observe my decrees" (Ezek. 36:27).

"I will make with them a covenant of peace; it shall be an everlasting covenant with them, and I will multiply them, and put my sanctuary among them forever" (Ezek. 37:26).

"The days are coming, says the Lord, when I will make a new covenant with the house of Israel and the house of Judah" (Jer. 31:31).

After the consecration of the bread and the wine, the Holy Spirit is called on for a second time: ". . . and by your Holy Spirit, gather all who share this one bread and one cup into the one body of Christ, a living sacrifice of praise." Saint Augustine said to recent converts of Hippo (Sermon 272), "Become that which you receive: the body of Christ."

It is the Holy Spirit who gives us the presence of Christ in the form of the bread and the wine of the Eucharist *and* in the reality of his ecclesial body, of which Christ is the head. In connecting in this way the sacrament, Body of Christ, and the Church, body of Christ, the Church proclaims that the Eucharistic Body, the "real presence" of Christ, is the sign and guarantee of his presence in the midst of the body of his Church.

If this were not true, the body would take itself for the head, the Church would take itself for Christ, the Bride for the Groom; and the Eucharist would not be the sacrament of living love, but only a nostalgic memory of a vanished presence.

The Church, the mystical body of Christ, does not worship itself, but worships Christ who is actually present in his Body and in his Blood that the Church receives in the sacrament of the Eucharist, which is its life.

*This is the Lamb of God
who takes away the sins of the world.
Happy are those who are called to his supper.*

13

COMMUNION

The Lord's Prayer

"Our Father, who art in heaven . . ."

The period or "moment" of Communion begins by the recitation of the Lord's Prayer. Communion is a private act in which each person receives the Body and Blood of Christ as nourishment. However, it is also an ecclesial act: with Christ, individual Christians become a single body united with all of the sons and daughters of our Heavenly Father.

To eat and drink of this true nourishment—"For my flesh is real food and my blood is real drink" (John 6:55)—forces us to make a realistic appraisal of our faith. In our human condition we are seized by the Spirit of the resurrected Christ, whose Body we eat and Blood we drink. Communion is a sharing of life, a "symbiosis." The life of Christ becomes our life, and our lives become the life of Christ.

Thus, in preparation for the paschal meal, which is to "eat his flesh and drink his blood" (cf. John 6:56), we enter into the prayer that Christ himself left us. It is the prayer of Christ the head that has become the prayer of his body, the prayer that is common to all the brothers and sisters of Jesus. Christ said, "My Father and your Father" (John 20:17), and he teaches us to say together with him "Our Father."

"Deliver us from evil . . ."

The final request of the Lord's Prayer is amplified by the insertion of a prayer of supplication composed in the fifth century by the Church of Rome, then a victim of barbarian invasions. "In your mercy keep us free from sin and protect us from all anxiety as we wait in joyful hope for the coming of our Savior, Jesus Christ." "Joyful hope" comes from an expression that Saint Paul used in his letter to Titus (2:13) when he speaks of "our blessed hope, the appearing of the glory of the great God and of our Savior Jesus Christ"– that is to say, our hope for the Day of Resurrection.

"Lord Jesus Christ, you said to your Apostles . . ."

Interrupting the prayer addressed to the Father, we turn ourselves toward Jesus, whom we are about to welcome in the act of Communion. We ask him for *his* peace: "Look not on our sins"–*my* sins–"but on the faith of your Church." Note that we do not say "my" faith or even "our" faith, which would mean the faith of a particular ecclesiastical community. It is only the faith of the entire Church, the Bride of Christ, that is worthy of the pardon asked for our sins and of the gift of the Body and Blood of Christ that we are about to receive.

". . . and grant us the peace and unity of your kingdom."

It is only Christ who is able to "gather into one all the dispersed children of God" (John 11:52). We pray to him, therefore, for the unity of his Church at the moment when we are about to partake of "the one bread, the one cup" (cf. 1 Cor. 10:16–17). We receive the Body of Christ, who is totally present in every fragment of the consecrated bread. The sacrament of the Eucharist fortifies and constructs the unity of the Church, which is the body of the resurrected Christ, because by his sacrifice on the cross, Christ triumphed over all division, that is to say, over death and sin.

The Sign of Peace

"The peace of the Lord be with you always. . . . Let us offer each other the sign of peace."

In exchanging the sign of peace, a custom dating from the early church, we are not sharing a personal peace, but the peace we receive from Christ. It is a precious gift that transforms us. When we are seized by the peace of Christ and united in a single body with those who are given to us as brothers and sisters, we become "artisans of peace."

Communion

After the litany of "Lamb of God," we pray in silence and express words of humility and hope before receiving Christ in the Eucharist: "Lord, I am not worthy to receive you, but only say the word and I shall be healed." Each person goes forward to commune according to the custom of the church and individual sensibilities: either in the mouth or by extending the hand, following a beautiful manner attributed to Saint Cyril of Jerusalem: "With your left hand, make a throne for the right hand which is about to receive the King; curve the palm of your hand into a hollow and receive the Body of Christ as you say 'Amen.'"